DEAR LORD,

WE COME TO YOU TODAY WITH HEARTS FULL OF HOPE AND FAITH. WE KNOW THAT YOU ARE OUR STRENGTH AND OUR STRONGHOLD, AND WE TRUST IN YOUR ABILITY TO GUIDE US AND PROTECT US.

WE ASK THAT YOU GIVE US THE STRENGTH AND COURAGE WE NEED TO FACE THE CHALLENGES OF DAILY LIFE. WE KNOW THAT WE ARE NOT ALONE, AND THAT YOU ARE ALWAYS WITH US, HOLDING US UP AND LIFTING US UP WHEN WE FALL.

HELP US TO TRUST IN YOUR PLAN FOR OUR LIVES, AND TO HAVE THE FAITH AND PERSEVERANCE WE NEED TO OVERCOME ANY OBSTACLE THAT COMES OUR WAY. GIVE US THE WISDOM AND DISCERNMENT WE NEED TO MAKE THE RIGHT CHOICES, AND TO KNOW WHEN TO LET GO AND WHEN TO HOLD ON.

WE ASK THAT YOU BLESS THIS JOURNAL, "FROM STRENGTH TO STRENGTH," AND ALL WHO WILL USE IT AS A TOOL FOR PERSONAL REFLECTION AND SPIRITUAL GROWTH. MAY IT BE A SOURCE OF INSPIRATION, GUIDANCE, AND HOPE FOR ALL WHO READ IT.

WE PRAY ALL THIS IN JESUS' NAME, AMEN.

FOR THE LORD GIVES WISDOM;
FROM HIS MOUTH COME KNOWLEDGE AND UNDERSTANDING.

LET NO ONE SEEK HIS OWN GOOD, BUT THE GOOD OF HIS NEIGHBOR.

DEAR LORD,

THANK YOU FOR YOUR GRACE AND FORGIVENESS. WE CONFESS THAT WE HAVE NOT ALWAYS BEEN FORGIVING TOWARDS OTHERS, AND WE ASK FOR YOUR HELP IN LETTING GO OF OUR RESENTMENT AND BITTERNESS.

GIVE US THE STRENGTH TO FORGIVE AS YOU HAVE FORGIVEN US. HELP US TO SEE OTHERS THROUGH YOUR EYES AND TO LOVE THEM AS YOU DO. WE PRAY FOR THE ABILITY TO EXTEND FORGIVENESS TO THOSE WHO HAVE HURT US, WHETHER INTENTIONALLY OR UNINTENTIONALLY.

AND WE PRAY FOR THE WISDOM TO KNOW WHEN TO FORGIVE AND WHEN TO SEEK RECONCILIATION. WE PRAY THIS IN JESUS' NAME. AMEN.

LOOK CAREFULLY THEN HOW YOU WALK, NOT AS UNWISE BUT AS WISE, MAKING THE BEST USE OF THE TIME, BECAUSE THE DAYS ARE EVIL.

IF ANY OF YOU LACKS WISDOM, LET HIM ASK GOD, WHO GIVES GENEROUSLY TO ALL WITHOUT REPROACH, AND IT WILL BE GIVEN HIM.

BUT THE WISDOM FROM ABOVE IS FIRST PURE, THEN PEACEABLE, GENTLE, OPEN TO REASON, FULL OF MERCY AND GOOD FRUITS, IMPARTIAL AND SINCERE.

HOW MUCH BETTER TO GET WISDOM THAN GOLD!
TO GET UNDERSTANDING IS TO BE CHOSEN RATHER THAN SILVER.

SAY NOT, "WHY WERE THE FORMER DAYS BETTER THAN THESE?"
FOR IT IS NOT FROM WISDOM THAT YOU ASK THIS.

WALK IN WISDOM TOWARD OUTSIDERS, MAKING THE BEST USE OF THE TIME.

LET YOUR SPEECH ALWAYS BE GRACIOUS, SEASONED WITH SALT, SO THAT YOU MAY KNOW HOW YOU OUGHT TO ANSWER EACH PERSON.

BY INSOLENCE COMES NOTHING BUT STRIFE,
BUT WITH THOSE WHO TAKE ADVICE IS WISDOM.

WHOEVER GETS SENSE LOVES HIS OWN SOUL;
HE WHO KEEPS UNDERSTANDING WILL DISCOVER GOOD.

IF ANYONE AMONG YOU THINKS THAT HE IS WISE IN THIS AGE,
LET HIM BECOME A FOOL THAT HE MAY BECOME WISE.

WHOEVER GUARDS HIS MOUTH PRESERVES HIS LIFE;
HE WHO OPENS WIDE HIS LIPS COMES TO RUIN.

SO TEACH US TO NUMBER OUR DAYS
THAT WE MAY GET A HEART OF WISDOM.

DEAR LORD,

WE COME TO YOU TODAY ASKING FOR WISDOM. WE KNOW THAT WISDOM COMES FROM YOU AND WE SEEK YOUR GUIDANCE IN ALL THAT WE DO. HELP US TO SEE THINGS FROM YOUR PERSPECTIVE AND TO UNDERSTAND YOUR WILL FOR OUR LIVES. GIVE US THE WISDOM TO MAKE GOOD DECISIONS, TO LEAD OTHERS WELL, AND TO LIVE OUR LIVES IN A WAY THAT BRINGS HONOR AND GLORY TO YOUR NAME.

WE PRAY THAT YOUR WISDOM WOULD GUIDE US IN OUR THOUGHTS, WORDS, AND ACTIONS. HELP US TO BE DISCERNING, TO UNDERSTAND WHAT IS RIGHT AND TRUE, AND TO ALWAYS CHOOSE THE PATH OF RIGHTEOUSNESS.

WE TRUST IN YOUR GOODNESS AND FAITHFULNESS, AND WE KNOW THAT YOU WILL GIVE US THE WISDOM WE NEED WHEN WE ASK FOR IT. THANK YOU FOR YOUR LOVE AND GRACE, AND FOR THE GIFT OF WISDOM.

IN JESUS' NAME, AMEN.

WHEN PRIDE COMES, THEN COMES DISGRACE,
BUT WITH THE HUMBLE IS WISDOM.

FOR WHOEVER FINDS ME FINDS LIFE
AND OBTAINS FAVOR FROM THE LORD.

THE FEAR OF THE LORD IS INSTRUCTION IN WISDOM,
AND HUMILITY COMES BEFORE HONOR.

A FOOL TAKES NO PLEASURE IN UNDERSTANDING,
BUT ONLY IN EXPRESSING HIS OPINION.

THAT THE GOD OF OUR LORD JESUS CHRIST, THE FATHER OF GLORY, MAY GIVE YOU THE SPIRIT OF WISDOM AND OF REVELATION IN THE KNOWLEDGE OF HIM.

THE WISE OF HEART WILL RECEIVE COMMANDMENTS,
BUT A BABBLING FOOL WILL COME TO RUIN.

THIS ALSO COMES FROM THE LORD OF HOSTS;
HE IS WONDERFUL IN COUNSEL
AND EXCELLENT IN WISDOM.

EVEN A FOOL WHO KEEPS SILENT IS CONSIDERED WISE;
WHEN HE CLOSES HIS LIPS, HE IS DEEMED INTELLIGENT.

WHOEVER IS SLOW TO ANGER HAS GREAT UNDERSTANDING,
BUT HE WHO HAS A HASTY TEMPER EXALTS FOLLY.

THE BEGINNING OF WISDOM IS THIS: GET WISDOM,
AND WHATEVER YOU GET, GET INSIGHT.

FOR IN MUCH WISDOM IS MUCH VEXATION,
AND HE WHO INCREASES KNOWLEDGE INCREASES SORROW.

BLESSED IS THE ONE WHO FINDS WISDOM,
AND THE ONE WHO GETS UNDERSTANDING.

THE FEAR OF THE LORD IS THE BEGINNING OF KNOWLEDGE;
FOOLS DESPISE WISDOM AND INSTRUCTION.

THE FEAR OF THE LORD IS THE BEGINNING OF WISDOM,
AND THE KNOWLEDGE OF THE HOLY ONE IS INSIGHT.

KNOW THAT WISDOM IS SUCH TO YOUR SOUL;
IF YOU FIND IT, THERE WILL BE A FUTURE,
AND YOUR HOPE WILL NOT BE CUT OFF.

HEAVENLY FATHER,

WE COME TO YOU TODAY WITH GRATEFUL HEARTS, THANKFUL FOR THE GIFT OF LIFE YOU HAVE GIVEN US. WE ACKNOWLEDGE THAT EVERY BREATH WE TAKE, EVERY STEP WE MAKE, IS A BLESSING FROM YOU. WE ARE HUMBLED BY YOUR LOVE AND GRACE THAT SUSTAINS US EACH DAY.

WE ASK FOR YOUR GUIDANCE AND WISDOM AS WE NAVIGATE THE UPS AND DOWNS OF LIFE. HELP US TO TRUST IN YOUR PLAN AND PURPOSE FOR OUR LIVES, EVEN WHEN THINGS ARE DIFFICULT. GIVE US THE STRENGTH AND COURAGE TO FACE ANY CHALLENGES THAT COME OUR WAY, KNOWING THAT YOU ARE ALWAYS WITH US.

WE PRAY FOR THOSE WHO ARE STRUGGLING, FOR THOSE WHO ARE IN PAIN, FOR THOSE WHO ARE FACING DIFFICULT SITUATIONS. WE ASK FOR YOUR HEALING AND COMFORT FOR THEM AND FOR THEIR FAMILIES.

WE GIVE YOU THANKS FOR THE BEAUTY AND WONDER OF THIS WORLD YOU HAVE CREATED, FOR THE LOVE AND SUPPORT OF OUR FAMILY AND FRIENDS, AND FOR THE COUNTLESS BLESSINGS YOU POUR OUT ON US EACH DAY.

WE ASK ALL THESE THROUGH JESUS CHRIST OUR LORD.

AMEN.

I HAVE TAUGHT YOU THE WAY OF WISDOM;
I HAVE LED YOU IN THE PATHS OF UPRIGHTNESS.

OH, THE DEPTH OF THE RICHES AND WISDOM AND KNOWLEDGE OF GOD! HOW UNSEARCHABLE ARE HIS JUDGMENTS AND HOW INSCRUTABLE HIS WAYS!

GET WISDOM; GET INSIGHT;
DO NOT FORGET, AND DO NOT TURN AWAY FROM THE WORDS OF MY MOUTH.

WHOEVER WALKS WITH THE WISE BECOMES WISE,
BUT THE COMPANION OF FOOLS WILL SUFFER HARM.

THE WORDS OF A WISE MAN'S MOUTH WIN HIM FAVOR,
BUT THE LIPS OF A FOOL CONSUME HIM.

THE FEAR OF THE LORD IS THE BEGINNING OF WISDOM;
ALL THOSE WHO PRACTICE IT HAVE A GOOD UNDERSTANDING.

WITH HIS MOUTH THE GODLESS MAN WOULD DESTROY HIS NEIGHBOR,
BUT BY KNOWLEDGE THE RIGHTEOUS ARE DELIVERED.

THE LAW OF THE LORD IS PERFECT,
REVIVING THE SOUL;

THE TESTIMONY OF THE LORD IS SURE,
MAKING WISE THE SIMPLE.

MY SON, IF YOUR HEART IS WISE,
MY HEART TOO WILL BE GLAD.

A FOOL'S LIPS WALK INTO A FIGHT,
AND HIS MOUTH INVITES A BEATING.

A FOOL GIVES FULL VENT TO HIS SPIRIT,
BUT A WISE MAN QUIETLY HOLDS IT BACK.

THE FATHER OF THE RIGHTEOUS WILL GREATLY REJOICE;
HE WHO FATHERS A WISE SON WILL BE GLAD IN HIM.

A FOOL DESPISES HIS FATHER'S INSTRUCTION,
BUT WHOEVER HEEDS REPROOF IS PRUDENT.

THE VEXATION OF A FOOL IS KNOWN AT ONCE,
BUT THE PRUDENT IGNORES AN INSULT.

DEAR LORD,

WE COME TO YOU TODAY WITH OPEN HEARTS, READY TO RECEIVE YOUR LOVE AND GRACE. WE KNOW THAT OUR HEARTS ARE OFTEN FILLED WITH NEGATIVE THOUGHTS AND EMOTIONS, AND WE ASK FOR YOUR FORGIVENESS AND HEALING.

WE PRAY THAT YOU WOULD RENEW OUR HEARTS, FILLING THEM WITH YOUR LOVE, JOY, PEACE, PATIENCE, KINDNESS, GOODNESS, FAITHFULNESS, GENTLENESS, AND SELF-CONTROL. HELP US TO LOVE OTHERS AS YOU HAVE LOVED US, TO FORGIVE AS YOU HAVE FORGIVEN US, AND TO SERVE OTHERS AS YOU HAVE CALLED US TO DO.

WE ASK FOR YOUR PROTECTION AND GUIDANCE FOR OUR HEARTS. HELP US TO GUARD OUR HEARTS AGAINST ANYTHING THAT WOULD LEAD US AWAY FROM YOU, AND TO KEEP OUR HEARTS FOCUSED ON YOU.

WE ALSO PRAY FOR THOSE WHO ARE STRUGGLING WITH PHYSICAL OR EMOTIONAL ISSUES RELATED TO THE HEART. WE ASK FOR YOUR HEALING AND RESTORATION FOR THEM AND THEIR FAMILIES.

WE GIVE YOU ALL THE PRAISE AND HONOR, AND WE TRUST IN YOUR LOVE AND FAITHFULNESS. AMEN.

FINE SPEECH IS NOT BECOMING TO A FOOL;
STILL LESS IS FALSE SPEECH TO A PRINCE.

A WISE SON MAKES A GLAD FATHER,
BUT A FOOLISH SON IS A SORROW TO HIS MOTHER.

SET YOUR MINDS ON THINGS THAT ARE ABOVE, NOT ON THINGS THAT ARE ON EARTH.

LOOK CAREFULLY THEN HOW YOU WALK, NOT AS UNWISE BUT AS WISE, MAKING THE BEST USE OF THE TIME, BECAUSE THE DAYS ARE EVIL.

YOU SHALL LOVE THE LORD YOUR GOD WITH ALL YOUR HEART AND WITH ALL YOUR SOUL AND WITH ALL YOUR MIND.

WHOEVER GETS SENSE LOVES HIS OWN SOUL;
HE WHO KEEPS UNDERSTANDING WILL DISCOVER GOOD.

THE PRUDENT SEES DANGER AND HIDES HIMSELF,
BUT THE SIMPLE GO ON AND SUFFER FOR IT.

IRON SHARPENS IRON,
AND ONE MAN SHARPENS ANOTHER.

KEEP YOUR HEART WITH ALL VIGILANCE,
FOR FROM IT FLOW THE SPRINGS OF LIFE.

AS IN WATER FACE REFLECTS FACE,
SO THE HEART OF MAN REFLECTS THE MAN.

YOU WILL SEEK ME AND FIND ME, WHEN YOU SEEK ME WITH ALL YOUR HEART.

CREATE IN ME A CLEAN HEART, O GOD,
AND RENEW A RIGHT SPIRIT WITHIN ME.

MAY HE GRANT YOU YOUR HEART'S DESIRE
AND FULFILL ALL YOUR PLANS!

TRUST IN THE LORD WITH ALL YOUR HEART,
AND DO NOT LEAN ON YOUR OWN UNDERSTANDING.

IN ALL YOUR WAYS ACKNOWLEDGE HIM,
AND HE WILL MAKE STRAIGHT YOUR PATHS.

DEAR LORD,

WE COME TO YOU TODAY ASKING FOR YOUR PROTECTION. WE KNOW THAT YOU ARE A SHIELD AROUND US, AND A STRONGHOLD IN TIMES OF TROUBLE. WE TRUST IN YOUR POWER AND LOVE TO KEEP US SAFE.

WE PRAY FOR PROTECTION FOR OURSELVES AND OUR LOVED ONES. SHIELD US FROM PHYSICAL HARM, EMOTIONAL HARM AND SPIRITUAL HARM. KEEP US FROM DANGER, ILLNESS AND EVIL.

WE PRAY FOR YOUR PROTECTION FOR OUR HOMES, OUR POSSESSIONS AND OUR COMMUNITIES. KEEP US SAFE FROM NATURAL DISASTERS, THEFT AND VANDALISM.

WE ASK FOR YOUR PROTECTION FOR THE VULNERABLE AMONG US: THE SICK, THE ELDERLY, THE HOMELESS, THE REFUGEE, AND THE PERSECUTED. BE THEIR SHELTER AND THEIR STRONGHOLD, AND GIVE THEM HOPE IN THE MIDST OF THEIR STRUGGLES.

WE KNOW THAT YOU ARE ALWAYS WITH US, AND THAT NOTHING CAN SEPARATE US FROM YOUR LOVE. WE TRUST IN YOUR GOODNESS AND FAITHFULNESS, AND WE GIVE YOU ALL THE PRAISE AND HONOR. AMEN.

YOU SHALL LOVE THE LORD YOUR GOD WITH ALL YOUR HEART AND WITH ALL YOUR SOUL AND WITH ALL YOUR MIND.

FOR WHERE YOUR TREASURE IS, THERE YOUR HEART WILL BE ALSO.

DELIGHT YOURSELF IN THE LORD,
AND HE WILL GIVE YOU THE DESIRES OF YOUR HEART.

A JOYFUL HEART IS GOOD MEDICINE,
BUT A CRUSHED SPIRIT DRIES UP THE BONES.

AND I WILL GIVE YOU A NEW HEART, AND A NEW SPIRIT I WILL PUT WITHIN YOU.

MY SON, DO NOT FORGET MY TEACHING,
BUT LET YOUR HEART KEEP MY COMMANDMENTS

THE WISE OF HEART WILL RECEIVE COMMANDMENTS,
BUT A BABBLING FOOL WILL COME TO RUIN.

BE STRONG, AND LET YOUR HEART TAKE COURAGE,
ALL YOU WHO WAIT FOR THE LORD!

HE HEALS THE BROKENHEARTED
AND BINDS UP THEIR WOUNDS.

WITH MY WHOLE HEART I SEEK YOU;
LET ME NOT WANDER FROM YOUR COMMANDMENTS!

LET THE WORDS OF MY MOUTH AND THE MEDITATION OF MY HEART
BE ACCEPTABLE IN YOUR SIGHT

BLESSED ARE THOSE WHO KEEP HIS TESTIMONIES,
WHO SEEK HIM WITH THEIR WHOLE HEART.

BLESSED ARE THE PURE IN HEART,
FOR THEY SHALL SEE GOD.

I WILL PRAISE YOU WITH AN UPRIGHT HEART,
WHEN I LEARN YOUR RIGHTEOUS RULES.

HOPE DEFERRED MAKES THE HEART SICK,
BUT A DESIRE FULFILLED IS A TREE OF LIFE.

HEAVENLY FATHER,

WE COME TO YOU TODAY ASKING FOR YOUR GUIDANCE AND WISDOM AS WE SEEK TO UNDERSTAND YOUR WORD. WE KNOW THAT YOUR WORD IS LIVING AND ACTIVE, AND WE DESIRE TO HAVE OUR HEARTS AND MINDS TRANSFORMED BY ITS TRUTH. OPEN THE EYES OF OUR UNDERSTANDING, THAT WE MAY SEE THE BEAUTY AND POWER OF YOUR WORD.

HELP US TO STUDY YOUR WORD DILIGENTLY AND WITH A TEACHABLE SPIRIT. GIVE US THE DISCERNMENT TO DISTINGUISH TRUTH FROM ERROR, AND THE HUMILITY TO SUBMIT TO YOUR WILL. FILL US WITH THE KNOWLEDGE OF YOUR TRUTH AND THE WISDOM TO APPLY IT TO OUR LIVES.

WE ASK THAT YOU WILL GIVE US THE COURAGE TO OBEY YOUR WORD, EVEN WHEN IT IS HARD OR UNCOMFORTABLE. WE PRAY THAT YOUR WORD WILL BE THE FOUNDATION OF OUR THOUGHTS AND ACTIONS, AND THAT IT WILL SHAPE THE WAY WE LIVE.

WE PRAY THIS IN THE NAME OF JESUS, WHO IS THE WORD MADE FLESH. AMEN.

SET ME AS A SEAL UPON YOUR HEART,
AS A SEAL UPON YOUR ARM

I HAVE STORED UP YOUR WORD IN MY HEART,
THAT I MIGHT NOT SIN AGAINST YOU.

YOUR TESTIMONIES ARE MY HERITAGE FOREVER,
FOR THEY ARE THE JOY OF MY HEART.

AND HOPE DOES NOT PUT US TO SHAME, BECAUSE GOD'S LOVE HAS BEEN POURED INTO OUR HEARTS THROUGH THE HOLY SPIRIT WHO HAS BEEN GIVEN TO US.

BUT I HAVE TRUSTED IN YOUR STEADFAST LOVE;
MY HEART SHALL REJOICE IN YOUR SALVATION.

MY SON, BE ATTENTIVE TO MY WORDS;
INCLINE YOUR EAR TO MY SAYINGS.

MY SON, IF YOUR HEART IS WISE,
MY HEART TOO WILL BE GLAD.

I WILL GIVE THANKS TO THE LORD WITH MY WHOLE HEART;
I WILL RECOUNT ALL OF YOUR WONDERFUL DEEDS.

THOUGH AN ARMY ENCAMP AGAINST ME,
MY HEART SHALL NOT FEAR

TEACH ME YOUR WAY, O LORD,
THAT I MAY WALK IN YOUR TRUTH;
UNITE MY HEART TO FEAR YOUR NAME.

THE PRECEPTS OF THE LORD ARE RIGHT,
REJOICING THE HEART;

THE COMMANDMENT OF THE LORD IS PURE,
ENLIGHTENING THE EYES.

ONLY FEAR THE LORD AND SERVE HIM FAITHFULLY WITH ALL YOUR HEART.

LET LOVE BE GENUINE. ABHOR WHAT IS EVIL; HOLD FAST TO WHAT IS GOOD.

LOVE IS PATIENT AND KIND; LOVE DOES NOT ENVY OR BOAST

LET ALL THAT YOU DO BE DONE IN LOVE.

"ALMIGHTY AND EVERLASTING GOD, CREATOR OF ALL THINGS AND SOURCE OF ALL LOVE, WE COME TO YOU IN HUMBLE FAITH. WE TRUST IN YOUR WISDOM, YOUR GOODNESS, AND YOUR MERCY. WE KNOW THAT YOU ARE ALWAYS PRESENT, ALWAYS LOVING, AND ALWAYS WORKING FOR THE GOOD OF ALL.

WE PRAY FOR AN INCREASE IN FAITH, THAT WE MAY TRUST IN YOU MORE FULLY AND FOLLOW YOU MORE CLOSELY. WE ASK THAT YOU WOULD GIVE US THE GRACE TO BELIEVE IN THE IMPOSSIBLE, TO TRUST IN YOUR PROMISES, AND TO WALK BY FAITH AND NOT BY SIGHT.

WE PRAY FOR THE GIFT OF FAITH, THAT WE MAY SEE THE WORLD THROUGH YOUR EYES AND KNOW THE TRUTH OF YOUR WORD. WE PRAY THAT WE MAY HAVE THE COURAGE TO STAND FOR WHAT IS RIGHT, THE STRENGTH TO PERSEVERE IN DIFFICULT TIMES, AND THE HOPE TO PERSEVERE IN THE FACE OF UNCERTAINTY.

WE ASK THAT YOU WOULD HELP US TO LOVE YOU MORE DEEPLY, TO SERVE YOU MORE WILLINGLY, AND TO FOLLOW YOU MORE CLOSELY.

WE PRAY THIS IN THE NAME OF YOUR SON, JESUS CHRIST, OUR LORD AND SAVIOR, AMEN."

LET ME HEAR IN THE MORNING OF YOUR STEADFAST LOVE,
FOR IN YOU I TRUST.

AND ABOVE ALL THESE PUT ON LOVE, WHICH BINDS EVERYTHING TOGETHER IN PERFECT HARMONY.

SO NOW FAITH, HOPE, AND LOVE ABIDE, THESE THREE; BUT THE GREATEST OF THESE IS LOVE.

WE LOVE BECAUSE HE FIRST LOVED US.

WITH ALL HUMILITY AND GENTLENESS, WITH PATIENCE, BEARING
WITH ONE ANOTHER IN LOVE.

ABOVE ALL, KEEP LOVING ONE ANOTHER EARNESTLY, SINCE LOVE COVERS A MULTITUDE OF SINS.

LET LOVE BE GENUINE. ABHOR WHAT IS EVIL; HOLD FAST TO WHAT IS GOOD.

THIS IS MY COMMANDMENT, THAT YOU LOVE ONE ANOTHER AS I HAVE LOVED YOU.

MAY THE LORD DIRECT YOUR HEARTS TO THE LOVE OF GOD AND TO THE STEADFASTNESS OF CHRIST.

LOVE ONE ANOTHER WITH BROTHERLY AFFECTION. OUTDO ONE ANOTHER IN SHOWING HONOR.

NO ONE HAS EVER SEEN GOD; IF WE LOVE ONE ANOTHER, GOD ABIDES IN US AND HIS LOVE IS PERFECTED IN US.

IF ANYONE SAYS, "I LOVE GOD," AND HATES HIS BROTHER, HE IS A LIAR; FOR HE WHO DOES NOT LOVE HIS BROTHER WHOM HE HAS SEEN CANNOT LOVE GOD WHOM HE HAS NOT SEEN.

GREATER LOVE HAS NO ONE THAN THIS, THAT SOMEONE LAY DOWN HIS LIFE FOR HIS FRIENDS.

THERE IS NO FEAR IN LOVE, BUT PERFECT LOVE CASTS OUT FEAR

YOU ARE PRECIOUS IN MY EYES,
AND HONORED, AND I LOVE YOU

OWE NO ONE ANYTHING, EXCEPT TO LOVE EACH OTHER, FOR THE ONE WHO LOVES ANOTHER HAS FULFILLED THE LAW.

AND MAY THE LORD MAKE YOU INCREASE AND ABOUND IN LOVE FOR ONE ANOTHER AND FOR ALL, AS WE DO FOR YOU.

WHOEVER PURSUES RIGHTEOUSNESS AND KINDNESS
WILL FIND LIFE, RIGHTEOUSNESS, AND HONOR.

ANYONE WHO DOES NOT LOVE DOES NOT KNOW GOD, BECAUSE GOD IS LOVE.

HATRED STIRS UP STRIFE,
BUT LOVE COVERS ALL OFFENSES.

YOU SHALL LOVE YOUR NEIGHBOR AS YOURSELF.' THERE IS NO OTHER COMMANDMENT GREATER THAN THESE.

MAY MERCY, PEACE, AND LOVE BE MULTIPLIED TO YOU.